Hold Your Horses

Nuggets of Truth
for People
Who Love Horses

...No Matter What

by Bonnie Timmons

WORKMAN PUBLISHING • NEW YORK

Cataloging-in-Publication Data is available from the Library of Congress.

ISBN 0-7611-1536-6

The author thanks *Practical Horseman Magazine*, where the following images first appeared: Pages 11, 15, 36, 37, 40, 45, 52, 56, 57, 60, 61, 63, 67, 78, 80, 86, 88, 95, 100, and 101.

Workman books are available at special discounts when purchased in bulk for premiums and sales promotions as well as for fund-raising or educational use. Special editions or book excerpts can also be created to specification. For details, contact the Special Sales Director at the address below.

Cover Design by Lisa Hollander

Workman Publishing Company, Inc.
708 Broadway
New York, NY 10003-9555

Printed in China
First printing April 2003

10 9 8 7 6 5 4 3 2 1

For Bill,
who always picks me up
and dusts me off

For their guidance and friendship,
I thank Joanne Palulian, Kay Dixon,
Lisa Brinton, Toni Mendez, Susan Bolotin
and, especially, Sally Kovalchick.
(And I can't forget Dozer,
who kept me in one piece...
mostly.)

TABLE of CONTENTS

1

FIRST LOVE

The first time you see a horse, you think:

(A) I want to take him home with me RIGHT NOW.

(B) This HUGE monster with sharp teeth and fire-breathing nostrils is going to EAT ME.

(A) Like him

(B) Don't

If you like horses, your life
changes forever. You can't sleep
or eat or be a very good cowgirl without
your trusty pal by your side
AT ALL TIMES.

If you don't like horses, you can save a lot of money and broken bones and take up something safe,

like dolls,

or

ROCK CLIMBING

Or extreme sports.

How to tell if you love horses

1. You feel sick. Do you feel well enough to go to school?
   ☐ No
   ☑ Absolutely not

2. Do you feel well enough to clean your room?
   ☐ No
   ☐ You gotta be kidding

3. Are you well enough to ride?
   ☐ Yes
   ☐ Of course
   ☐ Absolutely

Should you fall hopelessly in love with horses
your bedroom *SUDDENLY* houses
a thousand of them, all the
BEST.
They will soon stun the world by
winning every event,
always against impossible odds.

And when you smash tin cans
onto your feet, you can
clip-clop into the sunset.

If
you wish on every star
and beg your parents silly,
then maybe,

FINALLY,

you'll get to go
on a

PONY RIDE.

The Trail Ride

You live for trail rides, riding at the very end and holding back your pony

so when no one looks you can
GALLOP to catch up.

You love horses more than anything,
and draw them all over your folders and
notes, which you send, carefully folded,
to your best friend, who understands.

Finding an Instructor

It's easy, compared with finding room for
horses amid the sprawl.

Finding the Money

You spend every minute after school at a barn, mucking 20 stalls in exchange for one ride.

Finding the Nerve

EQUINOPHOBIA

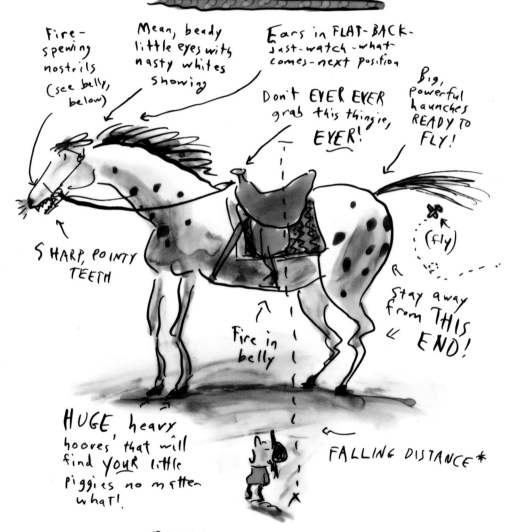

* Remember to RELAX while falling enormous distances.

Mounting the Insurmountable

By now you've learned that horses are
dangerous on both ends and uncomfortable
in the middle. That's why you CAN'T WAIT
to get started.

Getting On

1. Place mounting block beside the horse.

2. Stand on mounting block.

3. Watch horse move.

4. Move block to horse's new position.

5. Start to mount.

6. . . . .

...and when all else fails

7. Mount the
cowboy way.

The WHOA!

You WANT to GO
but first learn how to stop.

Bits help

Usually you
are just like a
flea, asking a
giant to STOP, PLEASE.

Excuse me, could you
PLEASE SLOW DOWN?

If you can't stop, but must, it is handy
to know the unscheduled dismount.

Whoa, Ol'
Spark plug

NOTE

Some horses do "whoa" well.
Others whoa only when they
want to whoa.

TIP
If vultures circle
overhead when you
ride, you need more
✧ giddy up. ✧

Giddy Up

The Basics

Gently ask your horse to
wake up. (He's a horse,
after all, and he has better
things to do.)

Give him a little nudge.
(Remind him you are
his VERY BEST friend.)

Go ahead – use your leg.
(Remind him it's a beautiful
day out there....)

Remind him who
FEEDS HIM.

OK. Grab that branch...

and tap him
just a bit....

Remember

Thank your pony
with a pat
and a "good boy"
when you
finally,
at long last,
catch him.

You are ready to ride. You know how to mount and how to whoa. Now you will learn about GAITS. If the gait you want is the gait you are getting, you are doing well.

The WALK

Sit DEEP

Sit DEEP in the saddle, take a deep breath, and RELAX, even though you know the ground is still far away and all hell could break loose any minute now.

uh-oh

Next, give your pony a gentle nudge and ask for the walk.

Some horses need more nudging than others.

Squeeze a little more, and you TROT. You will

The TROT

↑↓↑↓↑↓↑↓↑↓↑ ↑↓↑↓↑↓↑↓↑↓↑

In the trot, the ground is still far away,

only now it's moving away faster.

If you are riding western, sit deep in the saddle, relax, and become <u>ONE WITH THE HORSE.</u>

English riding, on the other hand, requires different techniques.

On some horses, this is especially difficult, but **THAT** is NO EXCUSE.

First, there is the sitting trot. Much like the western trot, there should be no air between you and your horse.

know you are trotting
if you jiggle all over.

squeezer muscles

You will discover
new muscles!

↑↓↑ ⬎↑↑↓ ↑ ↓ ↑↓ ↑↓↑ ↑↓ ↑ ↓↑⬎↑↑↓↑↑⬎↑↓↑

(your head remains level while
everything else
moves.)

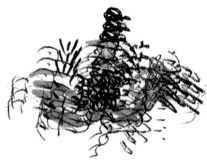

Then there is the rising trot,
also known as "posting" —
a smoothing out of the
ups and downs

This is something teachers
will make you do forever,
without stirrups.

The rising trot
should _NOT_ be confused
with the falling trot.

huh?

In this way you also become
one with the horse, until you start
to worry about diagonals. ⟶

Think diagonals are complicated? So do we. The diagonal is a concept that has something to do with trotting and posting. It makes no sense, and is far too complex to go into here - but this is the *diagonal essence* in a nutshell:

Diagonals*

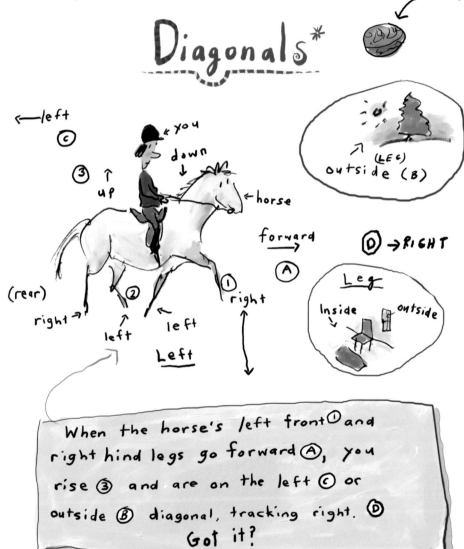

← left

ⓒ

③ ↑ up

← you

down ↓

← horse

forward →

Ⓐ

① right

(rear)

right →

② ↑ left

← left

Left

↗ (LEG) outside (B)

Ⓓ → RIGHT

Leg

Inside ↓   outside

When the horse's left front ① and right hind legs go forward Ⓐ, you rise ③ and are on the left ⓒ or outside Ⓑ diagonal, tracking right. Ⓓ
Got it?

*Always used with the word "WRONG!"

Squeeze a little harder and do another zillion things right and suddenly you will canter.

LESSON
8

The Canter

T a da rum, ta da rum, ta da rum tum tum

As carefree as riding a rocking horse
as long as you stay on*
and have the correct lead*
and don't break into a trot
on a perfectly collected horse
and a perfectly collected you
who remembered to shine your boots
and have no cares in the world
as long as he doesn't buck
and no one sees you peeking to
check your
leads →

*leads – similar to diagonals,
only different

The gallop happens on two occasions:
1) Suddenly you are COMPLETELY out of control
2) (Infrequent) You have asked your horse to gallop

The Gallop

It's REALLY FAST!

The gallop is a gait so fast,
your worries can't keep up.

But will he STOP?

☆ tip for staying on:
Just ride as fast
as he can run.

Sticking to the Saddle

Until you develop HUGE squeezer muscles,

will be tough.

TIP: Use everyday household helpers.

① Rub glue on your seat and boots.

(May not always work.)

② Apply Velcro to stirrups and soles.

(This, too, has drawbacks.)

MOMENTUM

A GOOD THING TO MAINTAIN

The single most important thing to remember when riding is to RELAX. The second most important thing to do is NEVER RELAX! Anything can happen. Large, scary things MIGHT cause your horse to stop. Suddenly.

(hey—if you wanted a sure Thing, you would have gotten roller skates)

momentum

For MOMENTUM, YOU may want to use AIDS ⟶

Aids are what you use to ask a horse to do something. They can be

NATURAL

hands
legs
seat
LouD growling noise
leg

OR ARTIFICIAL

spurs
crop

Or a large, mean, and nasty person with sharp teeth and a WHIP standing behind your sweet little horse. →

29

LESSON pre-13

NEXT, but not yet, comes JUMPING.

First, you must have a Low center of gravity,

not good ···>

<···· good

And a Good Seat,

legs too far forward

(Not like this, the "chair seat")

And have spent enough time trotting over and over and over and over poles on the ground.

Jumping

(A very silly thing to do, really)

head up
hands down
shoulders back
heels down
eyes up

MORE LEG →

three
TWO
ONE

Throw your
heart over
first....

After a thousand or so attempts, you
will begin to feel confident. Automatically,
you will remember to keep your heels
down, your head up, to look to the next fence,
lower your hands, steer, use EVEN MORE LEG,
come to the center of the fence, MORE LEG, MORE
LEG, relax, LEG, LEG, LEG, stay on, stay on, STAY ON,
and all the while, COUNT BACKWARD from three.

You will Feel Stupid.

In the beginning, say the first 30 years,
learning to ride will make you feel
like a dunce. This is because a horse
not only knows what you know, but
he also knows what you DON'T KNOW.

CONTINUING
EDUCATION

Pony Camp

Fun things you'll learn to do

Bareback dollar races

Spoon & egg race

Vaulting

Swimming

Costume Relays

A quiet moment

A 12-Step Program

1 It is good <u>not</u> to show a horse you are faint of heart.

You'll make him nervous.

A.

B.

C.

2

If you think your horse is REALLY COUNTING...

He's not. He's ROLLING.

Forget about having a good self-image.
You won't.

Sure, horses buck.
But often it means they
are feeling good. You should
be happy for them.

Girths are good;
you'll want one.

You will never win an argument with a
1,000-pound animal by using force.

At some point, you
will hit a ROADBLOCK.
Try a different direction for a while.

Whatever happens,
it is **ALWAYS**
the rider's fault.

9. Things Horses Shy At...

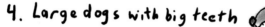

1. Lions in trees
2. Tigers anywhere
3. Helicopters
4. Large dogs with big teeth
5. Small dogs " " "
6. Dogs " " "
7. Dogs that weren't there yesterday
8. Rocks
9. Thermonuclear devices
10. Rogue nations
11. Plastic bags that flap
12. Bugs
13. Everything else

10. Things Horses Don't Shy at:

Falling

Old proverbs say
you MUST get
back on.
And on.

Call it an unscheduled dismount, and you'll
save face.

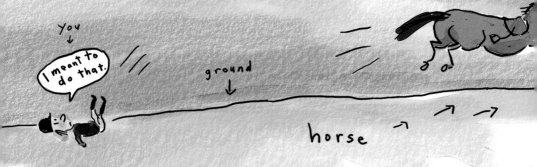

Lessons We forget to Remember

SAFETY TIPS

Riding is a VERY dangerous sport

Deus ex machina →

armor

auxiliary backup handle

parachute

Airbag

seat belt

Velcro saddle

short-legged horse for short falling distance →

↑ fluffy, soft landing material

The First Show

The day of showing begins very early.

TASKS

Mother	Child
1. Bathe horse with toothbrush.	
2. Clean tack with toothpick.	
3. Bathe child with patience.	
4. Pack SUV, load children, load pony...	
5. load pony, load pony...load pony...Leave.	
6. Return for fly spray and gloves.	
7. Arrive at show.	
8. Choose classes (mini-mini-mini or just mini-mini stirrup).	
9. Fill out form (while holding screaming kids and pony).	
10. Pay.	
11. Clean manure stains off pony from trailer.	
12. Dress child.	
13. Find missing boots.	
14. Find missing glove.	
15. Find missing child.	1. Ride.

But it's all WORTH IT in the end ———⟶

The children are crying,
either because they didn't win first place...

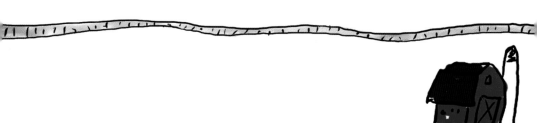

...didn't win even seventh place,

father
← holding
breath

parent →

...or because they won
a blue ribbon but their favorite
color is pink.

Then you'll need to translate between English- and Cowboy-speak.

DICTIONARY

HORSE- A big thing with four feet, eats hats. Can be ridden.

also, That which keeps your feet from touching the ground.

of ENGLISH and COWBOY terms

BUCK

1. buck

1. the kick of a beast with a belly full of springs 2. chinning the moon

CHAPS

1. (pronounced "chaps" as in "he's a good old chap") cool leather outfits for legs

1. (pronounced "shaps" for chaparral, prickly stuff that loves chapless legs) cool leather outfits for legs, with fringe

DOGGIE

1. a Jack Russell

1. (dogie) an orphaned calf — not a horse, not a little puppy

ENGLISH   COWBOY

HOME

East of the Mississippi to England, horses live in paddocks on farms.

West of there, they live in Pastures on ranches.

Longe*

(lunj) 1. taking the edge off a horse before riding by circling him until you fall down dizzy

1. getting the cayuse out of the pasture to ride

*not to be confused with "lounging"

ENGLISH | COWBOY

OUTFITS

1. rat catcher
2. formal attire
3. colors
4. silks
5. fine, expensive clothes—resembling mud in no time flat

1. boots greased and spurs shined
2. Sunday-go-to-meeting clothes—resembling mud at the git-go

SLOW

1. dead quiet

1. he couldn't even stop fast

SPURS

1. a pointy artificial aid

1. things that jingle jangle jingle

(a little) MORE~ COWBOY-HORSE

There are some terms that just don't translate.

(1) COW: Said by cowboys to be one of the dumbest creatures ever.

(2) Cowpony: A horse so bright, he can out-think a cow.

(3) Cowboy: One who can out think them both (on good days).

(4) Cuss: What cowboy lore says you do when you squat with your spurs on.

(5) Pee: What the late cowboy's horse stopped to do just before the Indians attacked

6 Rode hard and put away wet:
A very, very bad thing.
Cow boy loses all
his brownie
points.

7 Horse (cayuse)
What cowboys use
to keep their feet
from touching
the ground.

8 A hitch in your getalong:
You're off on the near fore.

9 The fall

1. cowboy sunned his moccasins
2. pickin' daisies
3. dirtied his shirt
4. grass hunting
5. a fartknocker
6. met his shadow on the ground

How to ride a horse:

Keep one leg on each side
and your mind in the middle

MORE LEARNING

You can learn much in clinics taught by pros.
Your horse, if you listen,
will teach you even more.

BUYING A HORSE

BUYING A HORSE

1 Finding the right horse will take LOTS of time and Lots of travel.

And did we mention money?

2 Always have the owner ride the horse first.

I usually just THINK "trot."

3 Make sure the horse can be caught <u>and</u> loaded into a trailer.

here, Tuffy

④ Notice the little things — that he doesn't bite, rear, stomp, buck, kick, or eat your bracelet.

(They only do these things to hear the funny noises that come out of us.)

Don't worry — if the horse doesn't work out, you can always sell him, right???

⑤ WRONG.
Remember,

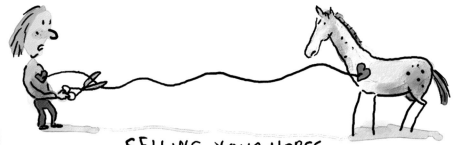

SELLING YOUR HORSE
will feel like selling a member
of your family.

The EVOLUTION OF THE HORSE

Before the
DAWN of MAN

Way Back When

The Dark Ages

Tinkering

Once the modern horse developed,
man started messing around
with evolution: breeding for different
colors, abilities, and personalities.

A while Ago Now Not Yet

Some combinations didn't work as well as others. Eventually we ended up with a huge range of horse types and breeds.

a horse that goes both ways

the horse for low openings

the six-cylinder horse

HORSES 4 SALE!

what they say
(and don't)

Has been
shown!

(came in last)

Jumps
4 ft!

Right out of his
pasture (daily)

QUIET –
walks, trots,
canters

But there's NO
stopping him
when he gets to
the gallop

FANCY PONY
Not for
beginner

or ANY child

X-race horse –
SOUND (when
he's not lame.)

Only gallops – to the
left – FAST.

BOMB
PROOF!

Won't move under
ANY circumstances

Fun to
ride !!!!.

If you are
a thrill
seeker

winning
bloodlines!

That SOMEHOW
didn't get passed
along

NO Vices

No virtues,
either

Choosing a BREED/TYPE

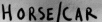

HORSE/CAR

Thoroughbred | Ferrari

FAST, sleek, a nice ride when not in the shop

Quarter horse | Pickup truck

Hardy, smart, utilitarian— a favorite of cowboys

Warmblood | Suburban

Roomy, comfy, gas guzzler; turning radius can improve

Arab | Land Rover

Good for the long haul, says **RUGGED**, with style

Pony | VW bug

Runs on practically nothing— good thing to have around for the kids - will still be around for THEIR kids.

Palomino | Chevy Impala

Pretty, if you like that sort of thing

Backyard cross | Old Volvo

Really safe, 100,000 miles and running great

miniature horse

Matchbox car

Eats less hay, gas

Within Breeds,
Even the Types Have Types

① The Comfy Horse

② The Evergreen
(Old enough to know
better)

③ The Very clever Pony
(Smart enough not to
pay attention to a child)

④

The free-to-a good-home, sadly-outgrown horse

⑤

The BIG, BOLD Horse

⑥ The complicated horse

⑦ The too-LARGE horse

⑧ The too-large rider

⑨ The mare

⑩ The Horse with personality

⑪ The Packer
(just gets the job done)

(12) The push-button horse

(13) The easy keeper

What Color?

Colors

Cowboy legend says Indians bred the sometimes stubborn Appaloosa so the warriors would arrive at battle fighting mad.

The Appaloosa was bred by the Nez Percé Indians who wanted a horse with camouflaging.

A paint or pinto also fades into its surroundings.

Gray horses are born black. Even a white horse is called a gray, as in "Look at that gray horse in the snowstorm."

Trying a New Horse

in front of absolutely everyone

You Find the PERFECT Horse!

Buying a Horse

The Rule of Tenths

Everyone involved takes a 10% cut, which is how a $3,000 horse ends up costing $20,000.

Now for the expensive part ⟶

Things You Will Need

1. STALLS *

Remember:
The number
of horses you
have will increase proportionately to the
number of stalls. Like magic!

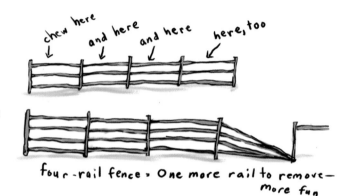

2. FENCES

Many styles,
all built to
give horses
something to
chew, remove,
or jump over

chew here ↓ and here ↓ and here ↓ here, too ↓

four-rail fence = One more rail to remove—
more fun

3. TACK ROOM

A place where
you find long-
lost items →

Inside
looks
something like this,↗
only messier.

4.

SOMEONE ELSE
Who will do all the
dirty work

*Don't confuse "stall" with what
your horse does when you say
"GO"

5. SADDLES

(you'll want one that fits)

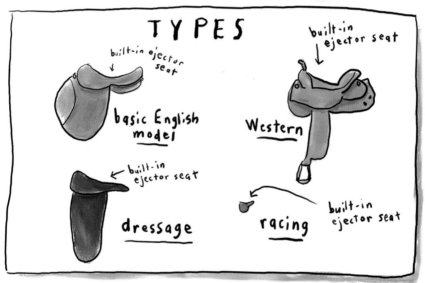

TYPES

basic English model
built-in ejector seat

Western
built-in ejector seat

dressage
built-in ejector seat

racing
built-in ejector seat

6. SADDLE PADS

They cushion like a mattress. →

clean area of peas for the princess first

7. BITS

A bridle can only properly be cleaned by disassembling it... ...which means reassembly must follow.

- Nasty—might as well beat a dead horse

- Not worth the horse you rode in on

- Complete with REAL carrot toy to amuse and distract

- designer wear

- just fine (if you like that sort of thing)

- platinum, but still turns slobbery green with wear

- fancy, straight from the horse's mouth

- really fancy, takes more than two hands to handle the reins

- tasty, green, won't hold your horses, though

8. NEW SHOES

Imagine buying two NEW PAIRS of shoes — expensive Italian types.

Now think of buying these two pairs every month for each of your horses.

9. OUTFITS

cut 'em out

Picture how you can look the part

Just something here

old barn coat

doesn't matter

(ALL put together with duct tape)

wellies

barn clothes

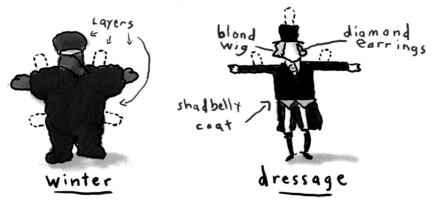

Layers

blond wig

diamond earrings

shadbelly coat

winter

dressage

stock tie

useless-but-fashionable top hat

flask (absolutely necessary for jumping)

R long, dangly crop

call it scarlet, call it pinque, but NEVER call it a "red" coat

The Hunt

SIX-shooter

Tuffy

Cowgirl

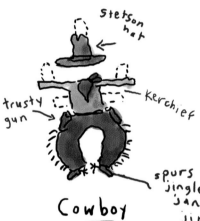

stetson hat

trusty gun

kerchief

spurs that jingle jangle jingle

Cowboy

Silver jewelry

silver

fringe gloves

fringe

tons of silver

more silver

Western Show Rider

muck →

barn coat →

← muck

muck boots →

← muck

Mucking

10. The Accessories

The well-dressed horse

earmuffs

little rubber bands

Woolly hood →

woolly winter coat

tail wrap

Water heater

ankle warmers

little cushy things

Studded snow shoes

WINTER

long mane for fly control

Fly mask (not a blind-fold) →

fly sheet

fly-proof leggings →

MICROMESH NO-FLY ZONE

flyswatter

sensible shoes

SUMMER

11. Don't forget your home

12. A PLACE FOR THE THINGS

The auxiliary tack box on wheels
(the car)

hay

top of the heap—
kids,
dog,
parent

bridle pieces
and spare bits

gum

saddles,
pads

dirty
towels

carrots,
an entry form.

dog
food,
cat,
Kleenex

chaps,
lunch,
spurs,
stock tie,
car bingo

halter,
tax returns,
seltzer water
bottles

homework,
crop,
boots

lowest layer— cell phone (ringing),
Game Boy, lunch

13. Next you will need a HORSE TRAILER.

The starter horse trailer

The when-did-I-get-all-these-horses trailer

The horse overenthusiast trailer

14. GIFTS

Mustn't forget the major holidays

CARE and FEEDING

CARETAKING

Some just throw out hay and water.
Others go to extremes.

YOUR TIME

FEEDING TIME

Before you know how much to feed your horse,
you'll first need to know how much
there is of him.

How to Weigh a Horse

① Weigh yourself.

② Weigh yourself holding the horse.

③ Subtract ① from ②.

Or try using the addition method.

You also need to know
HOW MANY
horses you have

How to Count Horses

1. Count the number of legs.
2. Divide by 4.

Once you know how many horses you have and what they weigh, you will know what it costs to FEED THEM.

(A lot)

What Your Horse Eats

GOOD FOOD	BAD FOOD
Hay	Earrings
Carrots, Apples	Necklaces
Oats	Things mistaken for carrots in men's pockets
Special Horse Nuggets	What you were about to eat

BATH TIME

Take a bucket
of water,

some soap,

a sponge

(does not have
to be "live");

add elbow grease

and a Flurry of Activity

to achieve this:

GROOMING

Before

After

After After

FLY-DEAD

HOOF GREASE

Sho-Sheen

tiny rubber bands →

horse cookies

Little Scratch Ointment

Big Awful Wound Unguent

Sheath Cleaner

↑
tick remover
(who can ever
find the
tweezers?)

FINDING YOUR NEW BEST FRIENDS

It's a good idea to
pamper your farrier. If you think
he was hard to find, he's harder to keep.
Go to extremes.

TROUBLESHOOTING

Six things that can go wrong*

1. Colic
Belly aches
and heartaches

2. Hoof Abscess
Foot aches
and more heartache

3. Spots
that weren't
there before

chicken
soup?

4. Upper respiratory infection
(a cold)

*Most are a long way from
the horse's heart, but awfully close to yours

5. The Three-Legged Horse

A You can make the horse stand
with his foot in a bucket of water.

1.   2.

B Or, stand there and hose the horse's leg
with cold water until <u>COMPLETELY</u> better.

OR, you can POULTICE.

Leg injuries take forever to heal, so they invented poultices to give you something to do to pass the time.

C The Poultice

1. Make a glop of hot, messy stuff.

2. Goop it onto horse's leg.

3. Cover with gauze.

4. And more gauze,

5. And more...

6. Wrap whole thing up with duct tape. REPEAT twice daily or Every time it all comes off.

6. Flies (TYPES of)

Little FLY

Big FLY

Fly-by-night

Shoe FLY

Dreaded Green head

Fly fishing

Fire FLY

Engine 23

blame all biting, kicking, bucking, and general ill will.

FLY in the ointment

Horse Fly

hola?

Spanish FLY

Good Fly

Fruit Fly

Pop FLY

Fly Mask

fly balls

One Fly too many ↗

(SEX)

Don't forget that horses are sexual beings.
You need to do something about it.
Ask your vet. Ask anyone.
Far too complicated to
go into here.

TRUTHS and CONSEQUENCES

Horsekeeping Truths

The neck of a horse is longest at medicine time.

If you are picking out his rear feet, then it's potty time.

The soundest horse will be lame the day you try to sell him.

Apples go into a horse well. They come out as drool, all over you.

If you are in your jammies, or running VERY late, the horse will NOT be caught.

Some horses have opposable lips and will pick any latch, bolt, or combination lock.

A clean stall will always be dirty in the morning.

The barn, of course, is spotless. YOU live in a three-bedroom, one-and-a-half-bath mudroom.

Truths

If you have one horse, you will need a second horse to keep it company.

If you have two horses and ride one, you'll need a third horse to keep company with the one left behind.

If you have three horses and ride two...

Flypaper sticks to MORE things than just flies.

Now that the stalls are clean and the horses fed and groomed, there is no time or energy left to ride.

After a long ride, the best rubbing post is the rider.

You can never disguise the fact you are a horseperson.

Now that you have all this, and all this has you, how can you ever leave home again?

BODY

Truths →

She'll be a STAR!
IDEAL
Blond hair
Itty bitty head
Sloping shoulders
absolutely no torso
Long legs
Low center of gravity
Born in the saddle

TYPES

To be really good, you need the right body.
To be good enough, you don't need a thing.

NOT

Center of
gravity at
nostrils

Big head

straight shoulders

Top-heavy →

LONG waist →

stubby legs

but the
dear _tries_ so
very hard

snap

Topples — just like that →

Truths

... sometimes the safety measures JUST DON'T WORK.

Anatomy of the Rider

(unlucky breaks)

Bees? Where?

WHO put that cow there?

oh, THAT'S what you meant by "DUCK"

What hole?

Is this the mare you said doesn't jump?

Whoa— WHOA... uh-oh

show-sheened horse, then galloped bareback

unscheduled dismount

found out horse doesn't do bounces

bad coop lousy crossrail BIG stake & bound evil oxer

Backed up too far at Big Cliff Overview

horse saw huge monster pretending to be a leaf

Was I following too closely to your mare in season?

Maybe we shouldn't have tried that jump one more time

Big, HUGE foot on teeny toes in flip-flops

Trailering
Truths

TWO THINGS that absolutely positively AREN'T TRUE

① That a horse EVER would willingly enter a trailer.

② That a driver could EVER drive backward to line up a teeny-weeny ball that can't be seen to an even smaller socket that is equally out of sight

Truths

Horses can sleep standing up. You can, too.
With a little help, of course.

HORSE PLAY
Things to do with your horse

Hacking and snacking

Bareback dips

Full moon rides

Chilling

Playing

Private moments of profound relaxation

HORSE SHOW

THE DRESSAGE

K

E

remember here to smile for the judge

A

Enter in control

Keep circles round

Gallop around some more here

Bumpy trot

F

FOX HUNTING

⏰ One fine day ⏰

1. Dress in old warm clothes,

2. embrace the day,

3. catch horse,

7. begin dressing,

8. tie stock tie...

9. ...tie stock tie,

12. drive to meet,

13. meet with decorum,

15. Ride like the wind. Remember why you love horses. Remember why you love life. Remember why the fox is spared so he can live to be chased again. (And to eat your pet chickens, and all their little baby McNuggets too, while he's at it.) 🐓 🐥 🐥 🐥 🐥

4. and groom,

5. defrost bit; tack up,

6. fill flask,

10. refill flask,

11. hook up trailer (allow 2 hours),

14. move off.

16. Awaken from reverie when horse loses shoe,

17. return home,

18. begin removing boots.

STEEPLECHASE

One of the more risky sports.
Requires nerves of steel, or so
many head injuries you don't know any better.

TAILGATE PARTIES

(only somewhat safer)

Consequences

At the End of the Day,

It's the warmth of a
steamy horse,

the feel of tired muscles,

the smell of clean stalls.

It's the sound of horses eating,

the sound of things you didn't hear,

and
knowing that when you
hold your horses,
they will hold you back.